# The Newbies: Bible Alphabets A–Z

*Activities and Coloring Book*

## BARBARA AND DENISE
# HENDRICKS

authorHOUSE®

*AuthorHouse™*
*1663 Liberty Drive*
*Bloomington, IN 47403*
*www.authorhouse.com*
*Phone: 1 (800) 839-8640*

*Published by AuthorHouse 09/07/2016*

*ISBN: 978-1-5246-1112-5 (sc)*
*ISBN: 978-1-5246-1111-8 (e)*

*Print information available on the last page.*

*Any people depicted in stock imagery provided by Thinkstock are models, and such images are being used for illustrative purposes only. Certain stock imagery © Thinkstock.*

*This book is printed on acid-free paper.*

# About the Authors

**<u>Barbara D. Hendricks</u>** is a writer and the owner of Broader Horizons Childcare & Development Inc. Barbara has owned her own daycare for 23 years and counting. She wanted to create a whole new children's book series that she could read to her new grandchildren and others. When they were born, God spoke to her and told her to write a children's book series. Barbara felt as if she had a new transformed life. Barbara D. Hendricks lives in Chicago, Illinois. She is a mother of four, a grandmother of 16 and counting, a foster parent for 22 years and counting. This children's book series is important to her because it reminds her of how much she loves to teach children. In her spare time, Barbara likes to help educate families on how to restore their credit.

**<u>Denise A. L. Hendricks</u>** is a loving and caring mother of 3. Denise loves to help others and is a Lifetime Girl Scout of Girl Scouts of Greater Chicago and Northwest Indiana. Denise loves to travel and help her community. She spending her time with her family and children. Denise's favorite things to do is read and spend time reading with her children.

What would you give to God?

ABEL

"The Lord respects ABEL's offering..." *Genesis 4:4 KJV*

ABEL

"El Señor ABEL ofreciendo respeto..." *Génesis 4:4 KJV*

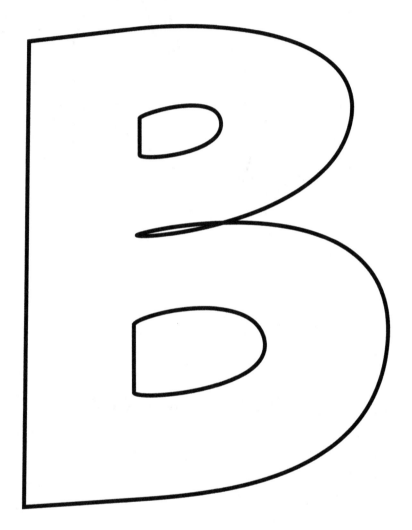

## BAPTIZE

"BAPTIZE you with water unto repentance..." *Matthew 3:11 KJV*

## BAUTIZO

"OS BAUTIZO con agua á arrepentimiento..." *Mateo 3:11 KJV*

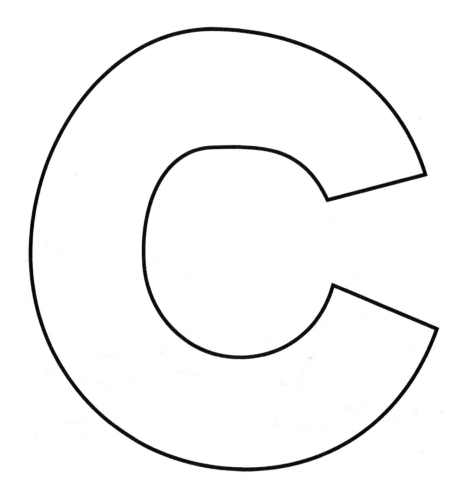

## COMMANDMENT

""These are the COMMANDMENTS, which the Lord commanded Moses for the children of Israel in Mount Sinai." *Leviticus 27:34 NIV*

## MANDAMIENTOS

"Éstos son los MANDAMIENTOS, que el Señor mandó (ordenó) a Moisés para los niños de Israel en Monte Sinai." *Leviticus 27:34 NIV*

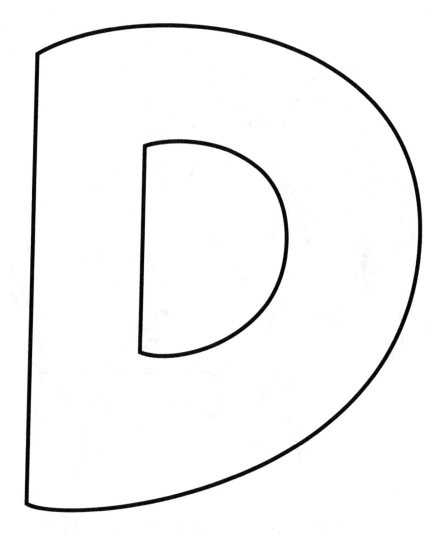

You are God's disciple.
Draw a picture of yourself!

## DISCIPLE

"If you hold to my teachings, you
are really my DISCIPLES..."
*John 8:31-32 NIV*

## DISCÍPULOS

"Si cumple con mis
enseñanzas, son realmente
mis DISCÍPULOS..."
*John 8:31-32 NIV*

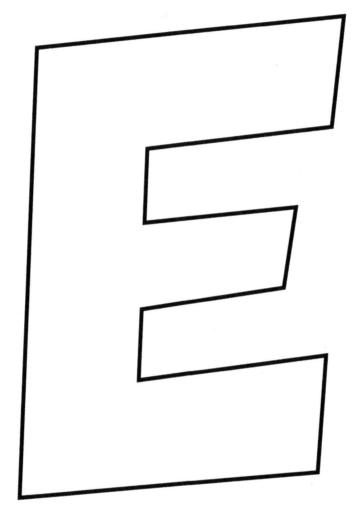

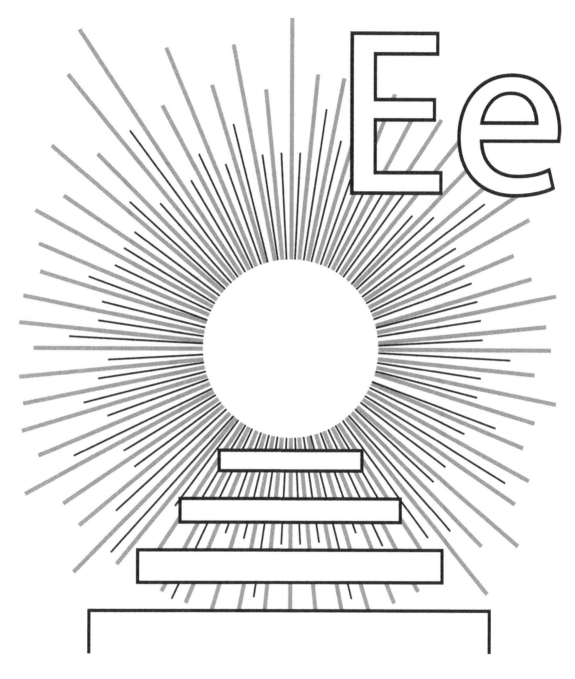

## ETERNAL

"Your word, Lord, is ETERNAL;
it stands firm in the heavens."
*Psalm 119:89 NIV*

## ETERNA

"Su palabra, Señor, es ETERNA;
se mantiene firme en el cielo."
*Salmo 119:89 NIV*

# FAITH

"FAITH is confidence in
what we hope for..."
*Hebrews 1:11 NIV*

# FE

"La FE es la confianza en
lo que se espera ..."
*Hebreos 1:11 NVI*

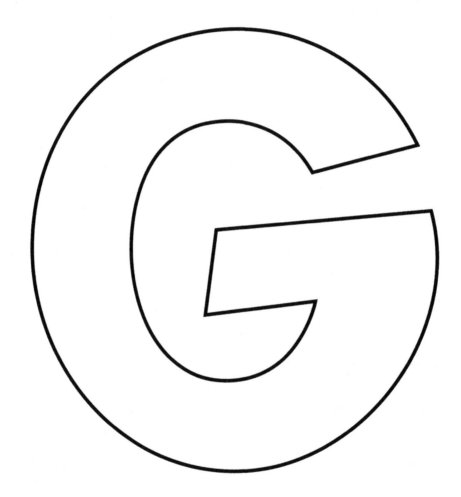

What does God look like? Draw the Lord!

GOD

"Blessed be the most high GOD..."
*Genesis 14:20 KJV*

DIOS

"Bendito ser DIOS más alto..."
*Genesis 14:20 KJV*

# HEAVEN

"In the beginning, God created
the HEAVEN and the earth."
*Genesis 1:1 KJV*

# CIELOS

"En el principio creó, Dios
los CIELOS y la tierra."
*Génesis 1:1 KJV*

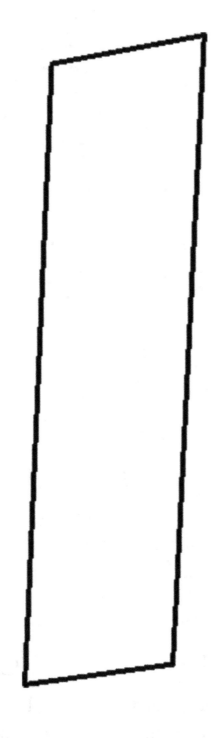

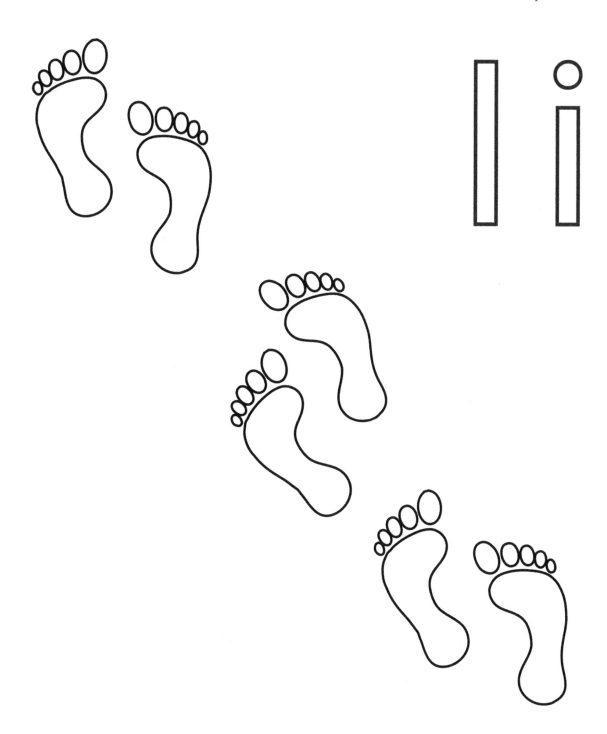

# INTEGRITY

"As for you, if you walk before
me in INTEGRITY..."
*1 Kings 9:4 NIV*

# INTEGRIDAD

"En cuanto a usted, si no anda antes
de mi en la INTEGRIDAD..."
*1 Reyes 9:4 NIV*

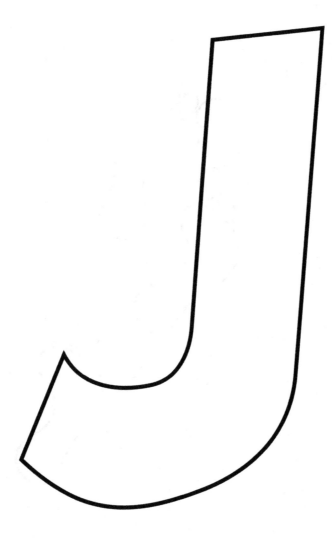

# Jj

## JESUS

"In the beginning of
the gospel about JESUS
Christ, the son of God."
*Mark 1:1 NIV*

## JESUCRISTO

"Al principio del evangelio sobre
JESUCRISTO, el hijo de Dios."
*Mark 1:1 NIV*

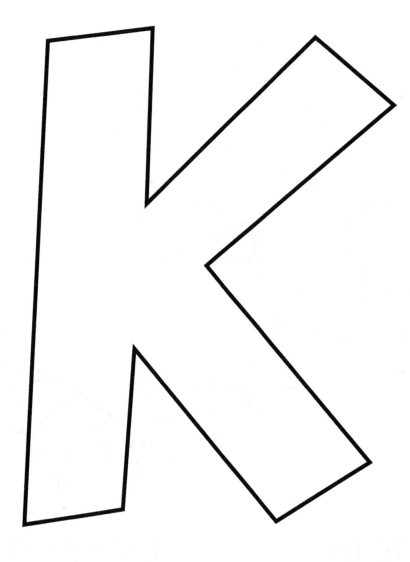

# Kk

KING

"KING of KINGS..."
*1 Timothy 6:15 KJV*

REY

"REY de REYES..."
*1 Timoteo 6:15 KJV*

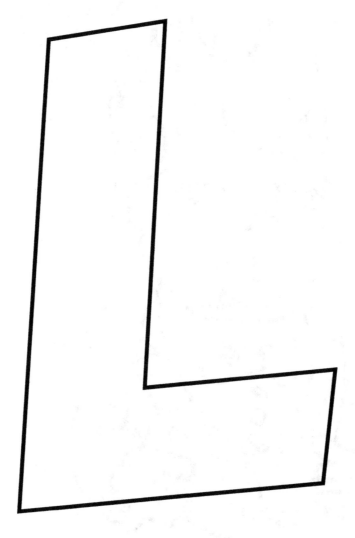

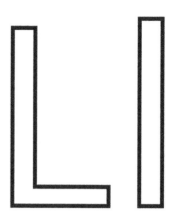

You are a Leader!
Draw a picture of a Leader.

## LEADER

"LEADER to people..."
*Isaiah 55:4 KJV*

## LÍDER

"LÍDER a la gente..."
*Isaías 55:4 KJV*

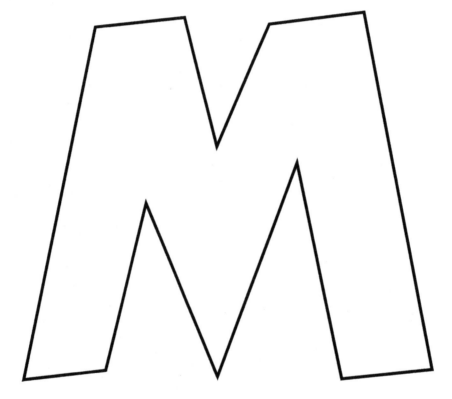

## MINISTER

"Elisha MINISTER to Elijah..."
*2 Kings 19:21 KJV*

## MINISTRO

"MINISTRO de Elisha a Elijah..."
*2 Reyes 19:21 KJV*

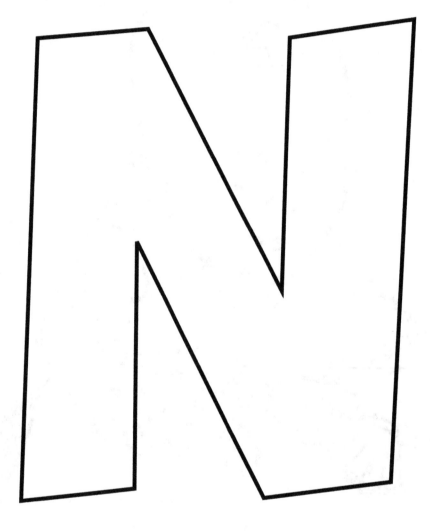

# Nn

## NATION

"An Holy NATION..."
*Exodus 19:6 KJV*

## NACIÓN

"Una NACIÓN Santa..."
*Éxodo 19:6 KJV*

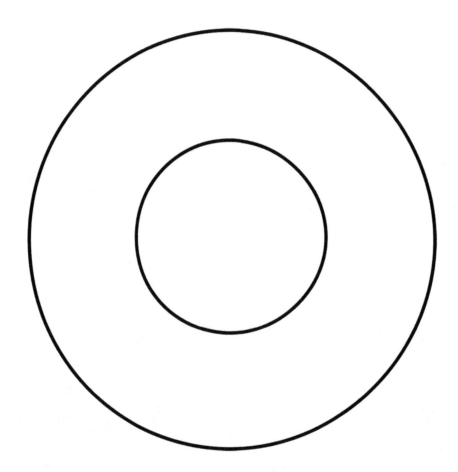

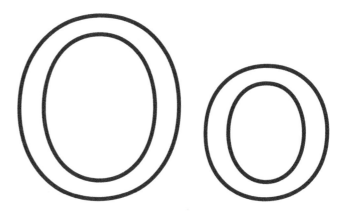

What would you offer to God?

## OFFERING

"Remember thy OFFERING..."
*Psalm 20:3 KJV*

## OFRECE

"Recuerde thy que OFRECE..."
*Salmo 20:3 KJV*

## PRAISE

"Singing PRAISES..."
*Judges 5:3 KJL*

## ALABANZAS

"Cantando ALABANZAS..."
*Jueces 5:3 KJL*

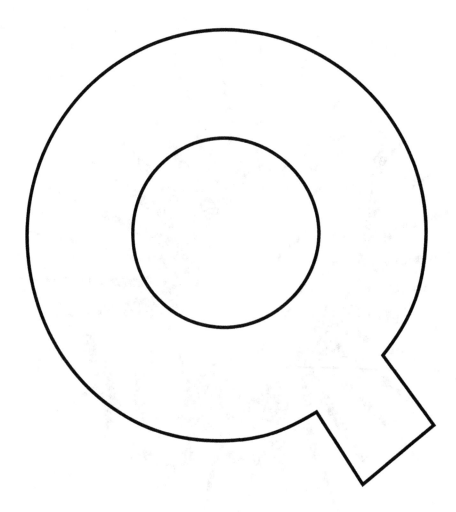

QUEEN

"QUEEN Esther..."
*Esther 7:1 KJV*

ALABANZAS

"La REINA Esther..."
*Esther 7:1 KJV*

## REPENT

"REPENT of sin..."
*Matthew 3:2 KJV*

## ARREPENTIRSE

"ARREPENTIRSE del pecado..."
*Mateo 3:2 KJV*

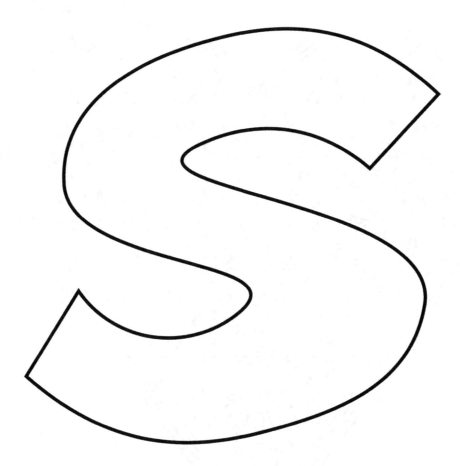

# Ss

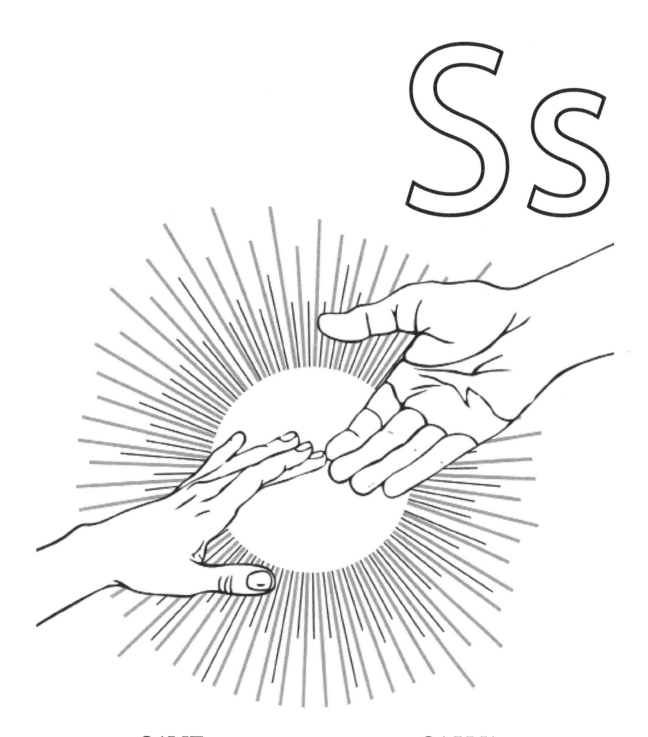

## SAVE

"SAVE your soul..."
*James 1:21 KJV*

## SALVA

"SALVA tu alma..."
*Santiago 1:21 KJV*

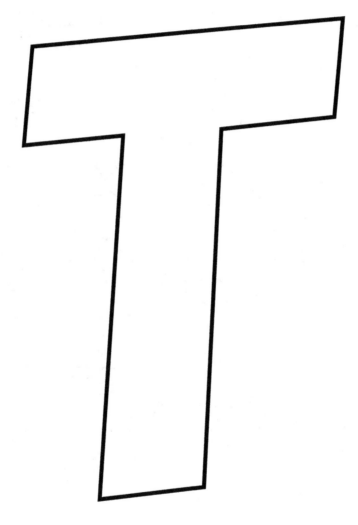

# TEMPTATION

"Lead us not into TEMPTATION"
*Matthew 6:13 KJV*

# TENTACIÓN

"Llévenos no a TENTACIÓN..."
*Mateo 6:13 KJV*

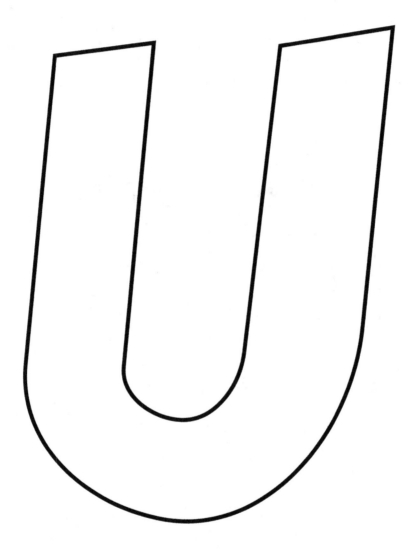

## UNCLEAN

"An UNCLEAN soul..."
*Leviticus 5:2 KJV*

## SUCIA

"Un alma SUCIA..."
*Leviticus 5:2 KJV*

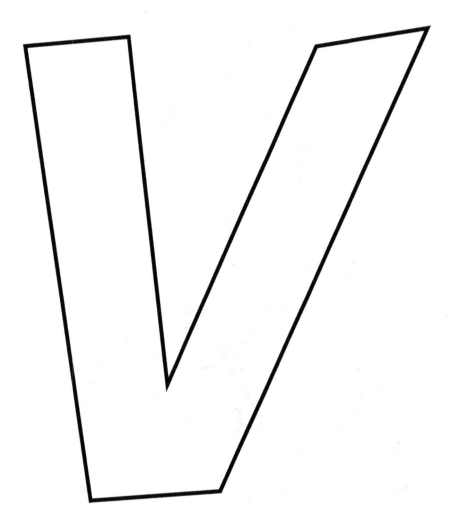

## VOW

""When you make a VOW to
God, do not delay to fulfill it..."
*Ecclesiastes 5:4 NIV*

## VOTO

"Cuando haces un VOTO a Dios,
no se demore para cumplirla..."
*Eclesiastés 5:4 NIV*

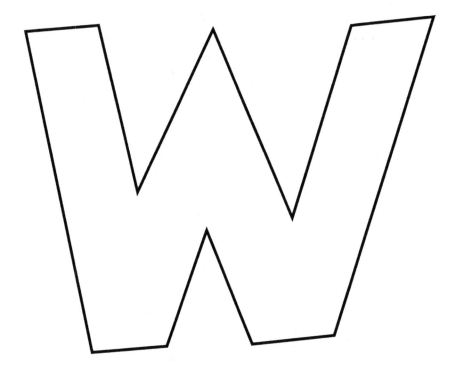

## WISDOM

"Glory and WISDOM..."
*Revelation 7:12 KJV*

## SABIDURIÁ

"Gloria y SABIDURÍA..."
*Revelación 7:12 KJV*

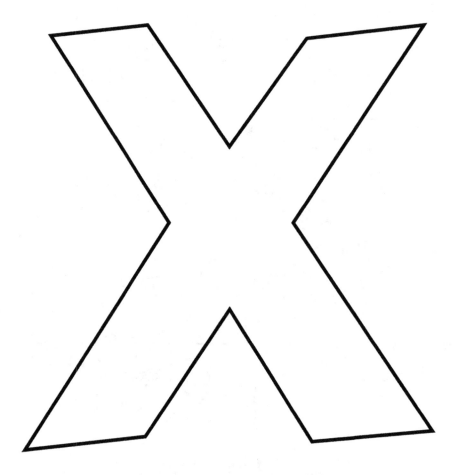

## XERXES

"XERXES loved Esther more
than any other women…"
*Esther 2:17 CEV*

## SABIDURIÁ

"XERSES amó a Esther más
que cualquier otra mujer…"
*Esther 2:17 CEV*

## YOKE

"Take my YOKE upon
you, and learn of me..."
*Matthew 11:29-30 KJV*

## YUGO

"Tome mi YUGO sobre
usted y aprenda de mí..."
*Mateo 11:29-30 KJV*

## ZEAL

"Have a ZEAL of God..."
*Romans 10:2 KJV*

## CELO

"Tienen un CELO de Dios..."
*Romanos 10:2 KJV*

# Connect the Dots!

1

8

4

5

2

3

6

7

# Connect the Dots!

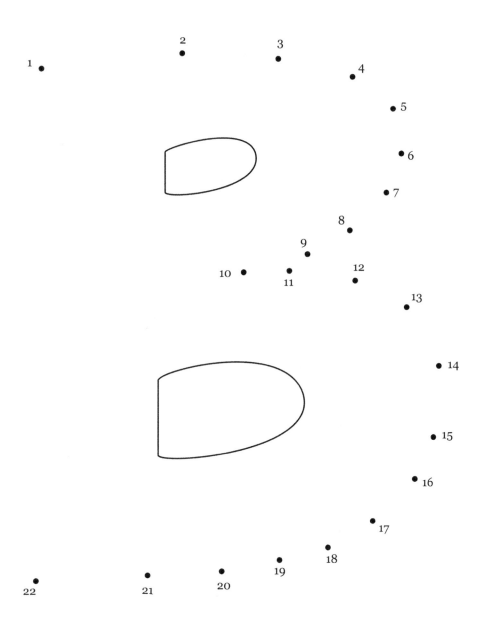

# Connect the Dots!

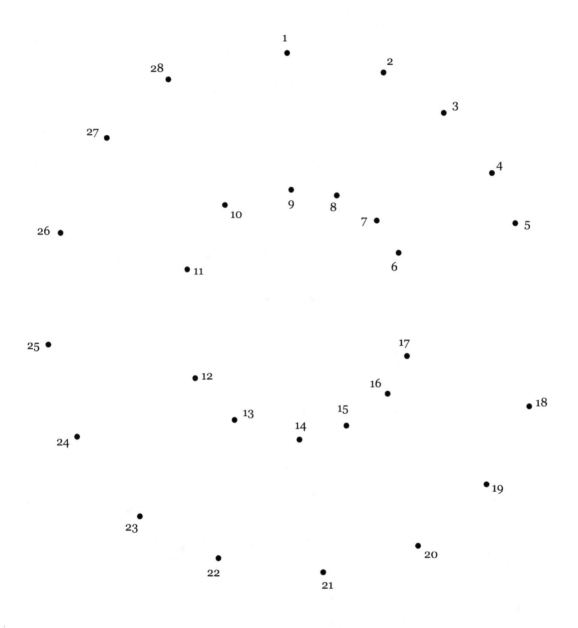

# Connect the Dots!

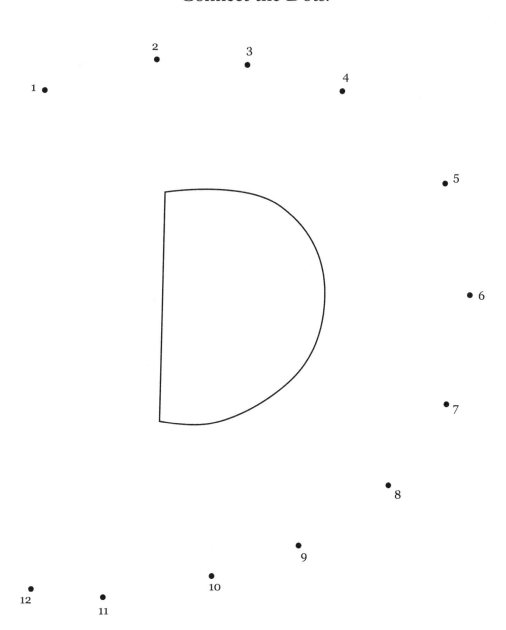

# Connect the Dots!

· 2

· 1

· 3

· 4

· 6

· 5

· 7

· 8

· 10

· 9

· 11

· 12

# Connect the Dots!

• 2

1
•

• 3

• 4

• 6

• 5

• 7

• 8

• 9

• 10

# Connect the Dots!

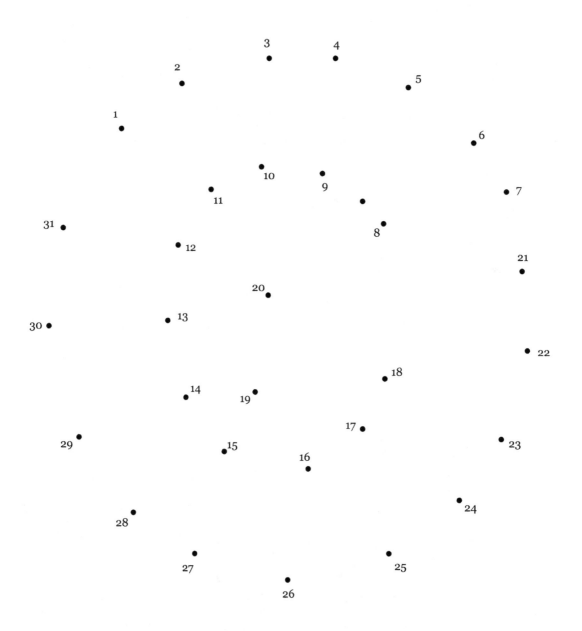

# Connect the Dots!

6
•

1
•

2
•

5
•

3
•

4
•

9
•

10
•

7
•

11
•

8
•

12
•

# Connect the Dots!

1
●

●2

●3

4●

# Connect the Dots!

1

2

15

3

14

10

11    12    13

4

9                    5

8

6

7

# Connect the Dots!

1
•

2
•

4
•

5
•

3
•

6
•

9
•

7
•

10
•

11
•

8
•

# Connect the Dots!

1

2

3

4

5

6

# Connect the Dots!

5

1 • 2 • 4 •

3 •

8 •

10 •

12 • 11 • 9 • 7 • 6 •

# Connect the Dots!

5

1 •

2 •

4 •

8 •

3 •

6 •

10 •

9 •

7 •

# Connect the Dots!

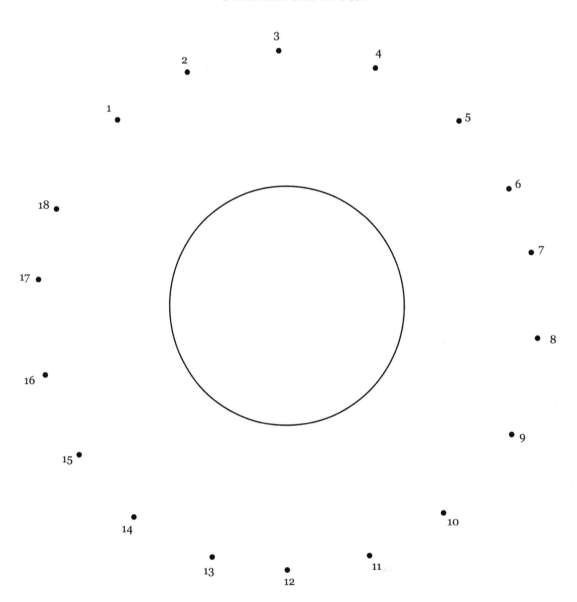

# Connect the Dots!

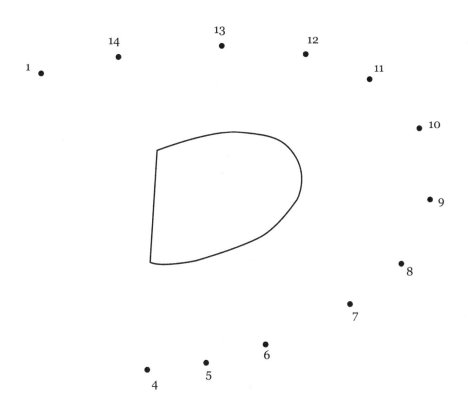

14

13

12

1

11

10

9

8

7

6

5

4

3

2

# Connect the Dots!

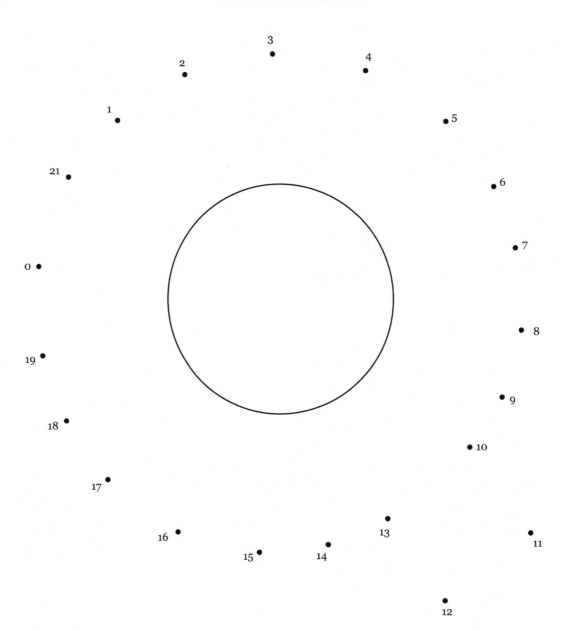

# Connect the Dots!

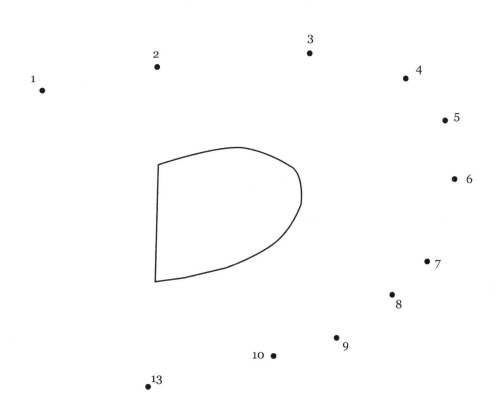

# Connect the Dots!

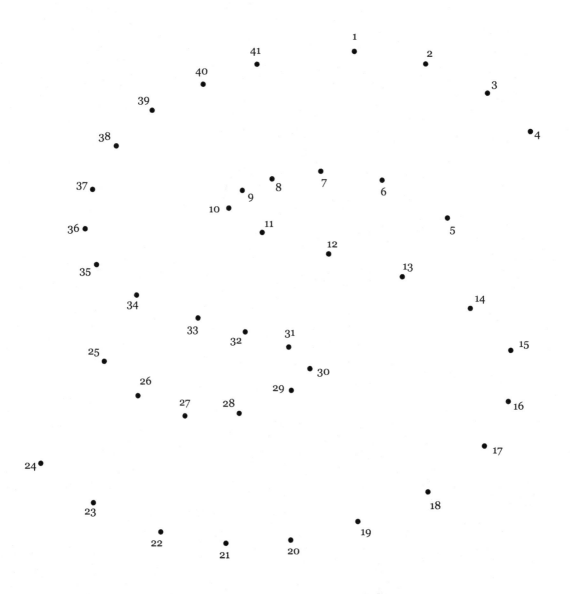

# Connect the Dots!

2 •

1
•

• 3

• 4

8 •

7 •

• 5

6 •

# Connect the Dots!

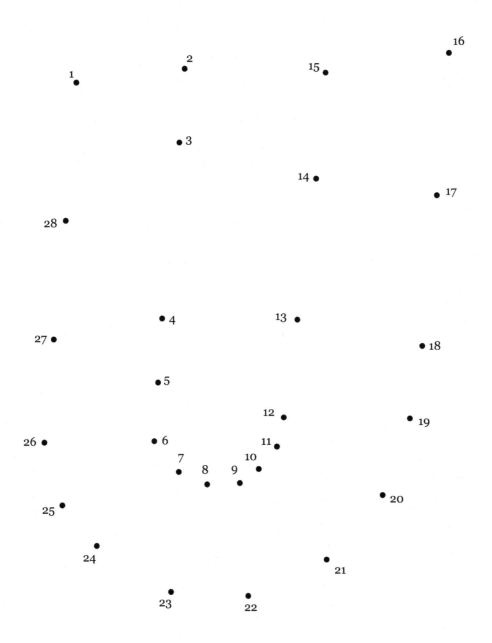

Connect the Dots!

1 •

2 •

6 •

7 •

3 •

5 •

8 •

11 •

4 •

10 •

9 •

# Connect the Dots!

1 •

2 •

4 •

8 •

9 •

5 •

10 •

7 •

16 •

3 •

13 •

6 •

11 •

14 •

12 •

15 •

# Connect the Dots!

12 •

1 •

3
•

•4

2 •

11 •

• 5

8 •

9 •

• 6

7 •

10 •

# Connect the Dots!

1 •

2 •

4 •

5 •

3 •

9 •

6 •

7 •

8 •

# Connect the Dots!

• 2

1
•

• 3

• 9

•
10

• 5

4 •

8 •

• 6

7 •

# To God Be the Glory

<u>**Other Books by The Newbies:**</u>

The Newbies: Bible Alphabets A-Z
The Newbies (coming soon)


Barbara D. Hendricks
Co-Author Denise A.L. Hendricks
Editor April M. Hendricks
Cory C. Hendricks

Jay
Paris
Gabby
Gia

To Contact us at the_newbies@yahoo.com. Follow us on twitter @_TheNewbies, Facebook @ TheNewbies, Instagram@_thenewbies. Check out our website www.newbiesseries.com.

The Newbies Organization
P.O.Box 63
Hazel Crest, IL 60429

Printed in the United States
By Bookmasters